SAM SMITH   THE THRILL OF IT ALL

2   TOO GOOD AT GOODBYES

8   SAY IT FIRST

13   ONE LAST SONG

18   MIDNIGHT TRAIN

23   BURNING

28   HIM

32   BABY, YOU MAKE ME CRAZY

37   NO PEACE

44   PALACE

48   PRAY

54   NOTHING LEFT FOR YOU

68   THE THRILL OF IT ALL

60   SCARS

64   ONE DAY AT A TIME

ISBN 978-1-5400-1568-9

HAL•LEONARD®

7777 W. BLUEMOUND RD. P.O. BOX 13819 MILWAUKEE, WI 53213

In Australia Contact:
Hal Leonard Australia Pty. Ltd.
4 Lentara Court
Cheltenham, Victoria, 3192 Australia
Email: ausadmin@halleonard.com.au

Visit Hal Leonard Online at
www.halleonard.com

TOO GOOD AT GOODBYES

Words and Music by SAM SMITH,
TOR HERMANSEN, MIKKEL ERIKSEN
and JAMES NAPIER

Pop Ballad

You must think that I'm stu - pid.

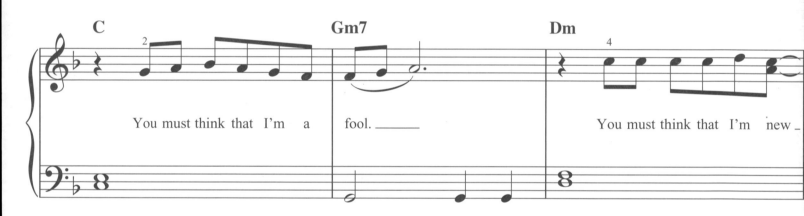

You must think that I'm a fool. You must think that I'm new

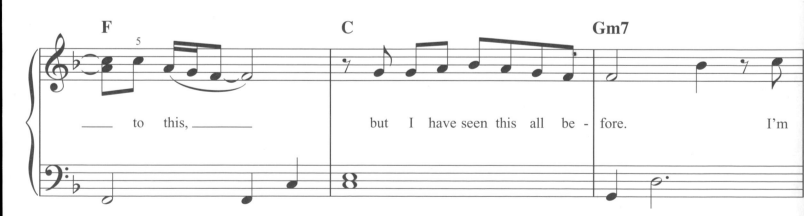

to this, but I have seen this all be - fore. I'm

nev-er gon-na let you close to me, e-ven though you mean the most to me. 'Cause

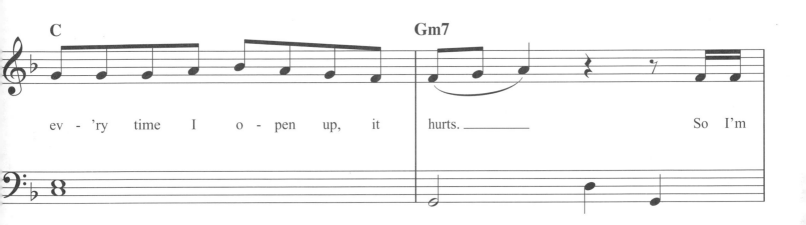

ev-'ry time I o-pen up, it hurts. _____ So I'm

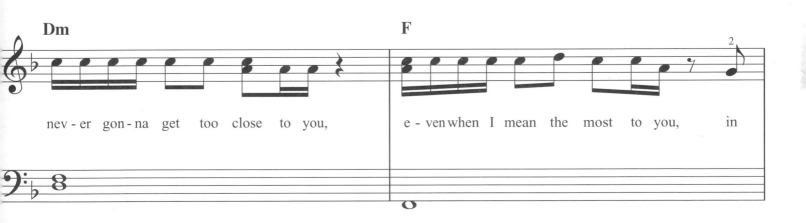

nev-er gon-na get too close to you, e-ven when I mean the most to you, in

case you go and leave me in the dirt. But ev-'ry time you

hurt me, the less that I cry. ___ And ev-'ry time you leave me, the quick-er these tears ___

___ dry. And ev-'ry time you walk out, the less I love you. ___

___ Ba - by, we don't stand a chance; it's sad but it's true. ___

___ I'm way too good at good-byes. ___ (I'm way too good at good-byes.)

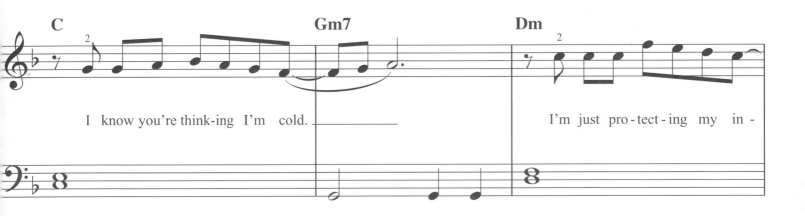

CODA · Gm7 · Dm

No way that you'll see me cry. ___ (No way that you'll see me cry.)

F · C · Gm7

I'm way too good at good-byes. (I'm way too good at good-byes.) ___

Dm · F

I'm way too good at good-byes. ___
No way that you'll see me cry. ___

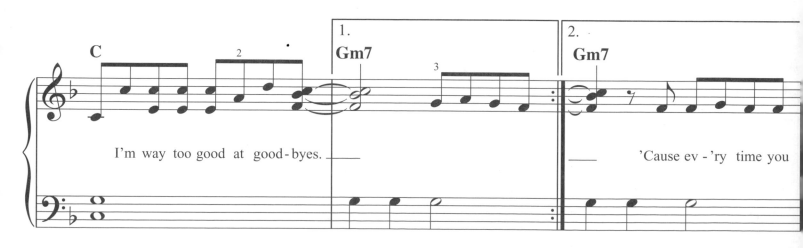

C · 1. Gm7 · 2. Gm7

I'm way too good at good-byes. ___ · 'Cause ev-'ry time you

hurt me, the less that I cry. _____ And ev - 'ry time you

leave me, the quick - er these tears _____ dry. And ev - 'ry time you

walk out, the less I love you. _____ Ba - by, we don't stand a

chance; it's sad but it's true. _____ I'm way too good at good - byes. _____

SAY IT FIRST

Words and Music by SAM SMITH,
JAMES NAPIER and JAMES RYAN WUIHUN HO

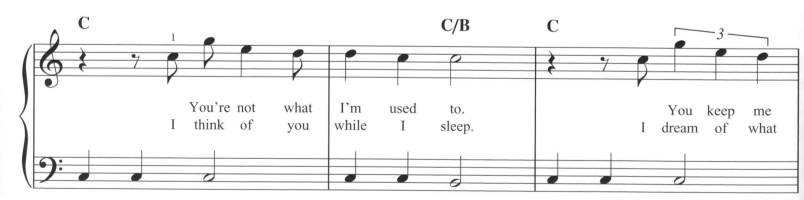

I need to hear you say those words___ if I'm all that you de-

sire,___ I prom-ise there'll be fire.___ I need to hear you

say it first.___ Come on, ba-by,___ do your worst.___ I know you'll take me___

To Coda

___ high-er.___ So come on, dar - ling, if you love me, say it first.

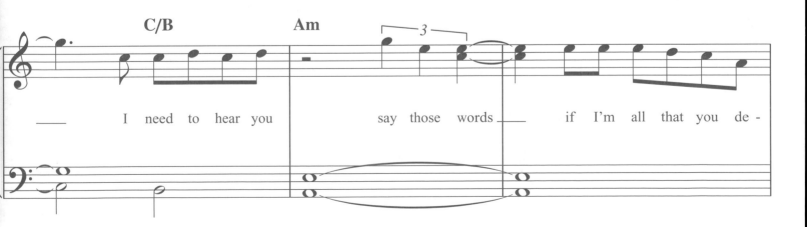

D.S. al Coda

sire, _____ I prom-ise there'll be fire. _____ I need to hear you

CODA

me, say it first. _____ (Say it, say it, say it. Won't you say it to me?

Say it, say it, say it. Won't you say it to me? Say it, say it, say it.

Won't you say it to me? Say it, say it, say it. Won't you say it to me?) _____
rit.

ONE LAST SONG

Words and Music by SAM SMITH,
JAMES NAPIER, TYLER JOHNSON
and CHARLES EMANUEL SMALLS

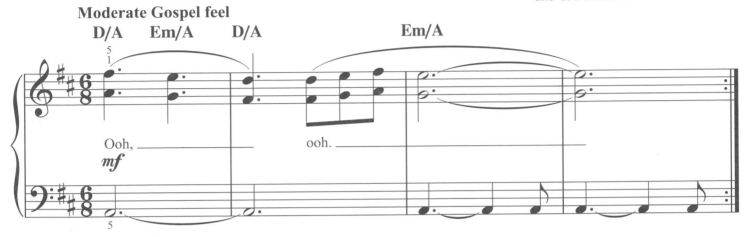

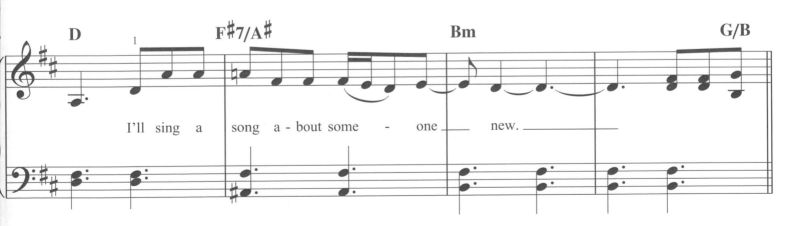

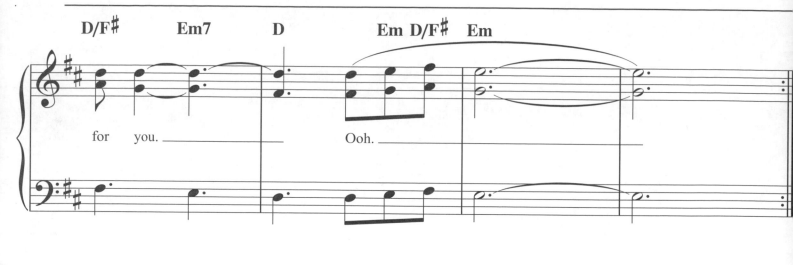

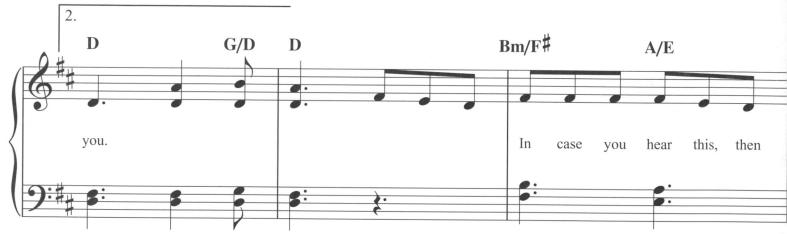

MIDNIGHT TRAIN

Words and Music by SAM SMITH
JAMES NAPIER and JAMES RYAN WUIHUN HO

train. I've got my rea-sons, but dar-ling, I can't ex-plain. I'll al-ways

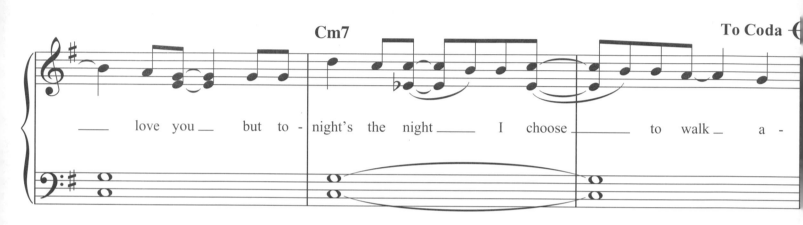

love you but to-night's the night I choose to walk a-

way. Ba ba do. Ba ba do. Ba ba do. Ba ba do.

So I pick up the piec - es, I get on a mid - night train. I've got my rea - sons,

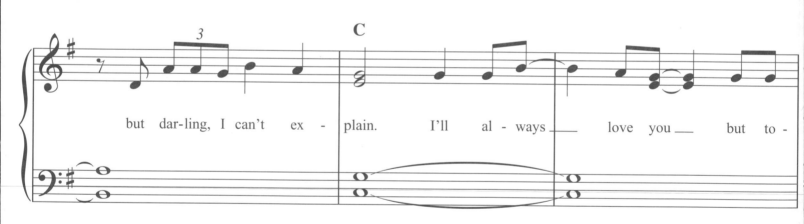

but dar-ling, I can't ex - plain. I'll al - ways ___ love you ___ but to -

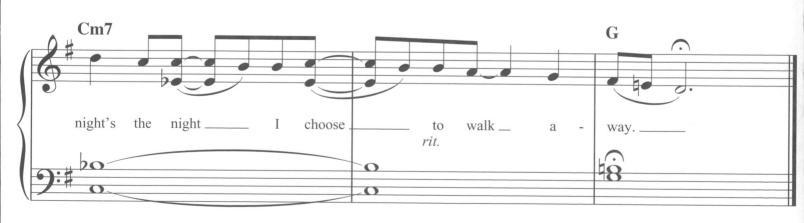

night's the night ___ I choose ___ to walk ___ a - way. ___

BURNING

Words and Music by SAM SMITH,
JASON BOYD, DOMINIC JORDAN
and JIMMY GIANNOS

Moderately

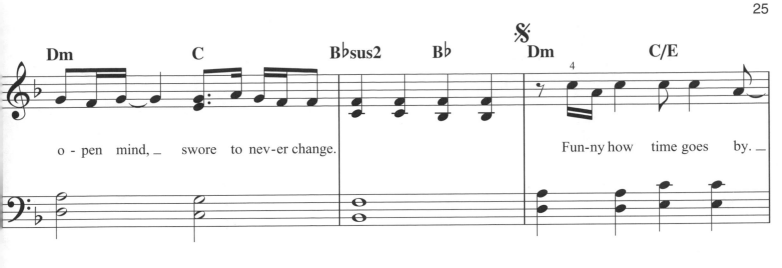

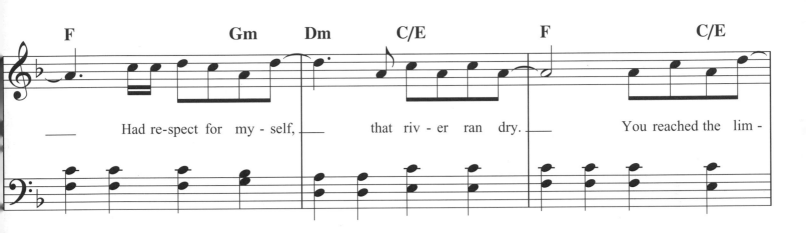

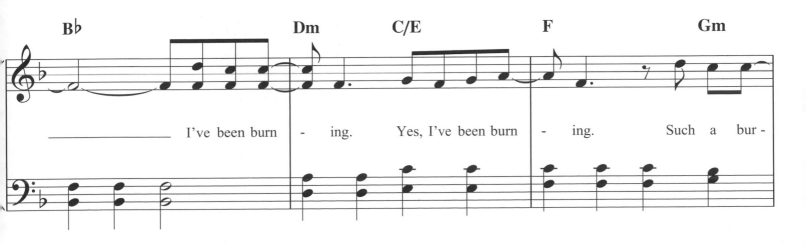

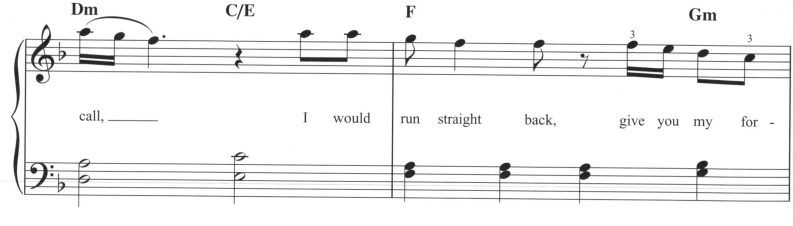

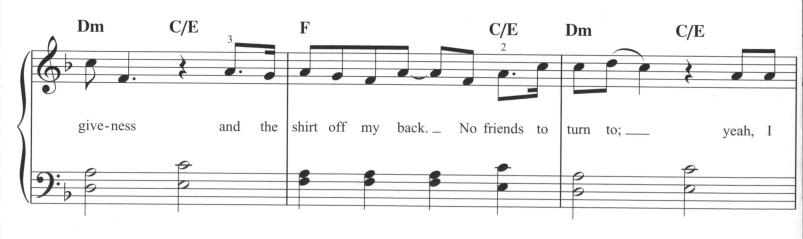

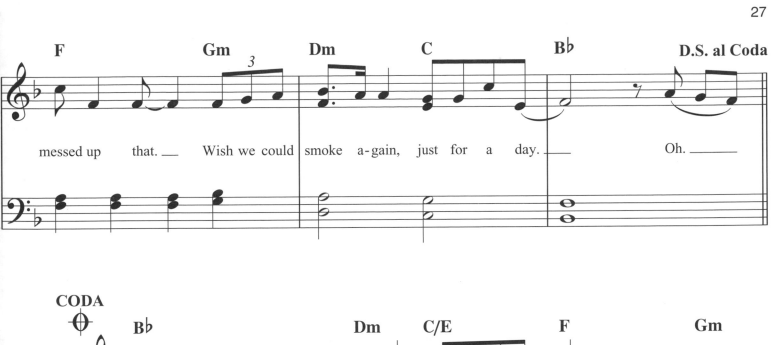

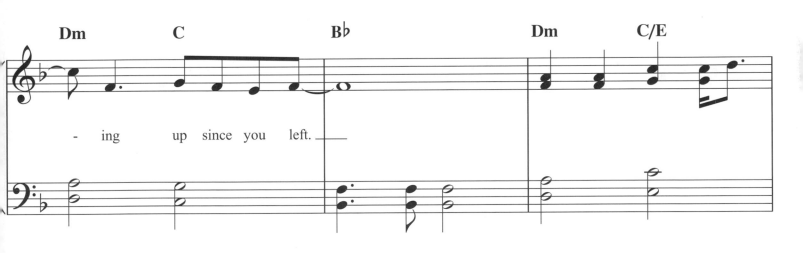

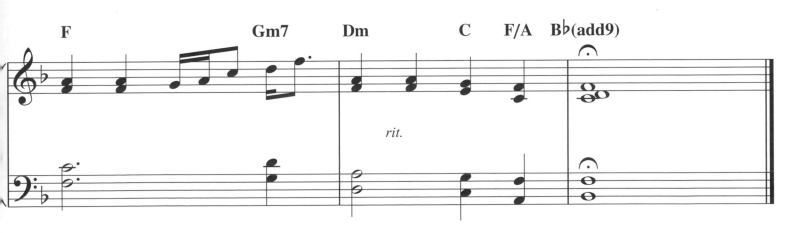

HIM

Words and Music by SAM SMITH,
BRENDAN GRIEVE and REUBEN JAMES

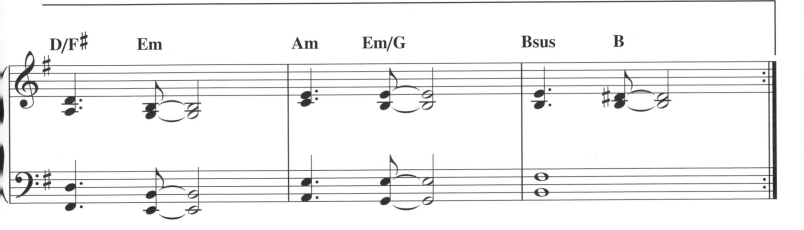

BABY, YOU MAKE ME CRAZY

Words and Music by SAM SMITH,
JAMES NAPIER, EMILE HAYNIE, DENNIS THOMAS,
WOODROW SPARROW, GENE REDD SR., GEORGE BROWN,
CLAYDES SMITH, RICHARD WESTFIELD, ROBERT BELL,
ROBERT MICKENS and RONALD BELL

With a smooth groove

says no? _____ Boy, get your-self to-geth - er, move __ on with your

life. So I'm gon - na play my fa - v'rite rhy - thm, ___ got to get you

out my sys - tem. __ I would do an - y - thing __ to keep you off my mind. I'm gon-na have to

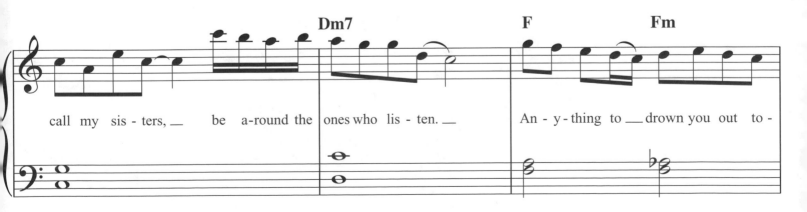

call my sis - ters, __ be a-round the ones who lis - ten. __ An - y - thing to __ drown you out to-

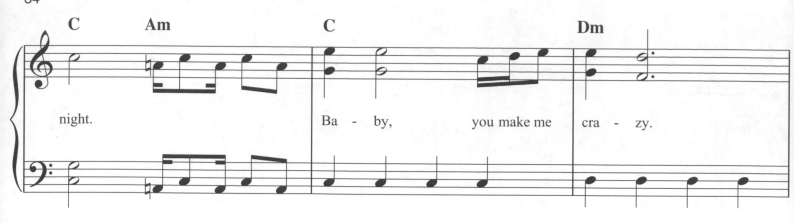

night.   Ba - by,   you make me   cra - zy.

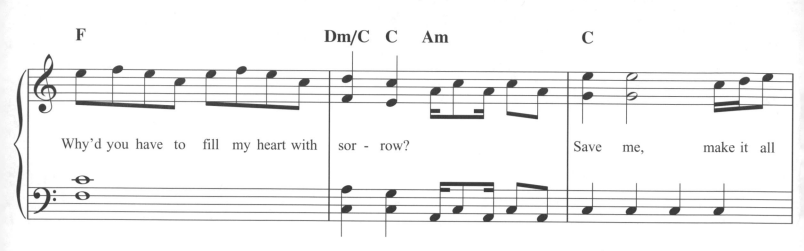

Why'd you have to fill my heart with   sor - row?   Save me,   make it all

To Coda ⊕

ha - zy   so   I don't think a - bout you till to - mor - row.

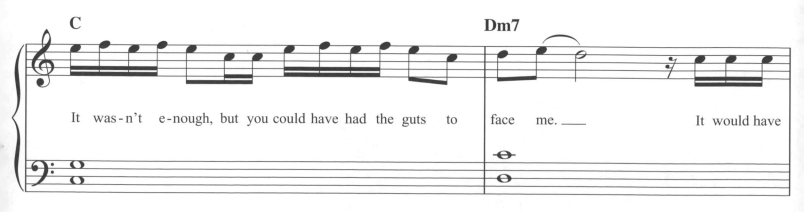

It was-n't e-nough, but you could have had the guts to   face me. ___   It would have

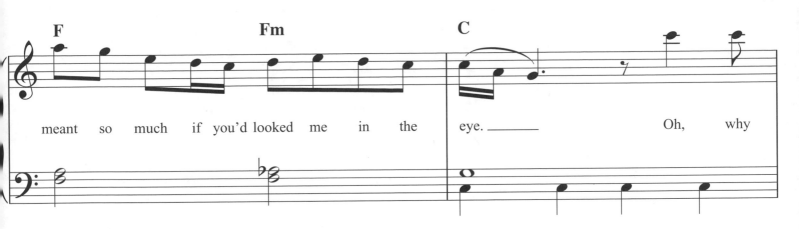

meant so much if you'd looked me in the eye. _____ Oh, why

do I al - ways fall for the ones who have no cour - age? __ I must

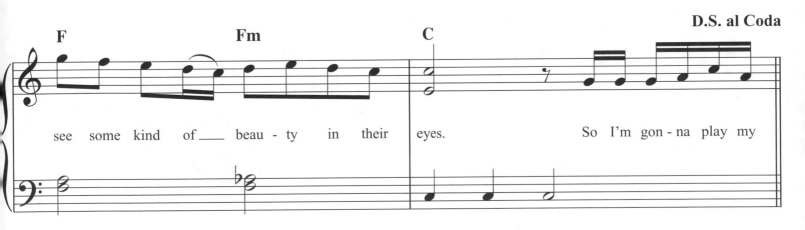

see some kind of ___ beau - ty in their eyes. So I'm gon - na play my

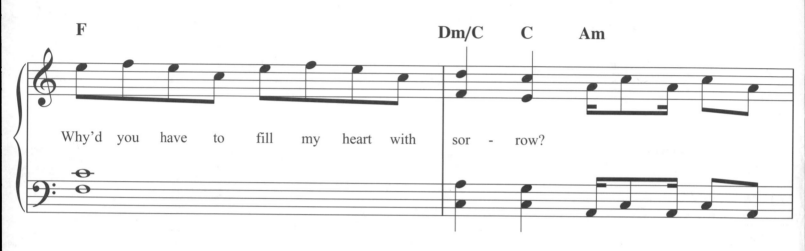

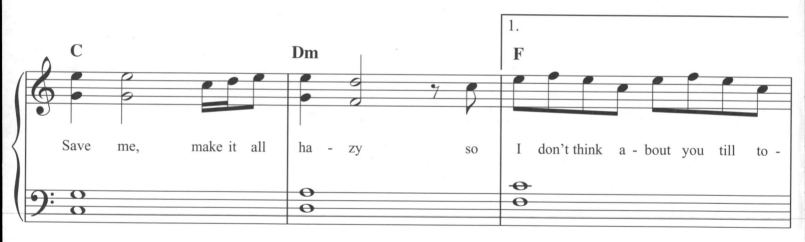

NO PEACE

Words and Music by SAM SMITH,
JAMES NAPIER and ABBEY SMITH

Moderate Ballad

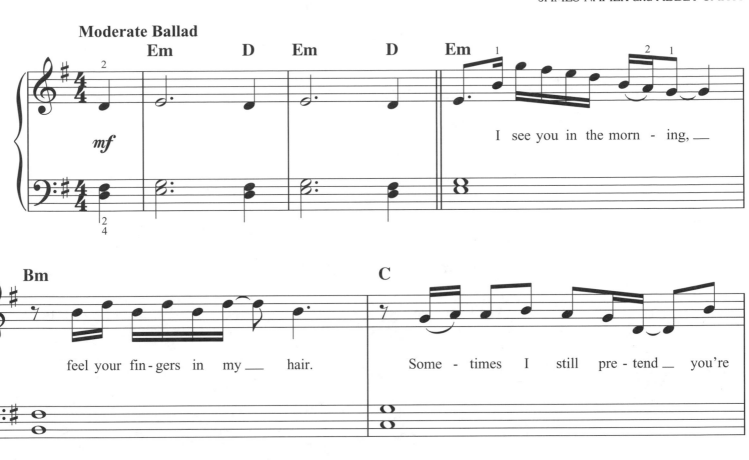

I see you in the morn - ing, ___

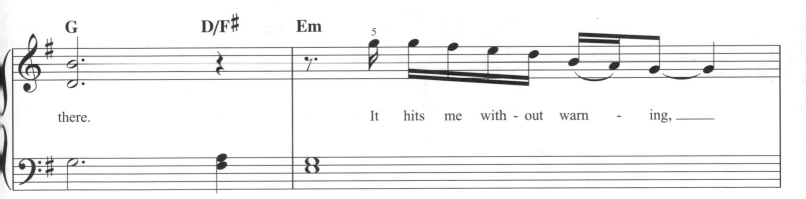

feel your fin - gers in my ___ hair. Some - times I still pre - tend ___ you're

there. It hits me with - out warn - ing, ___

your re - flec - tion walk - ing ___ by. But I know ___ it's on - ly in ___ my

mind.   Will you show ___ me the piece __ of my heart __ I've been miss - ing?

___   Won't you give ___ me the part __ of my - self __ that I can't give

back? _____   Will you show ___ me the piece __ of my heart __ I've been miss - ing? __

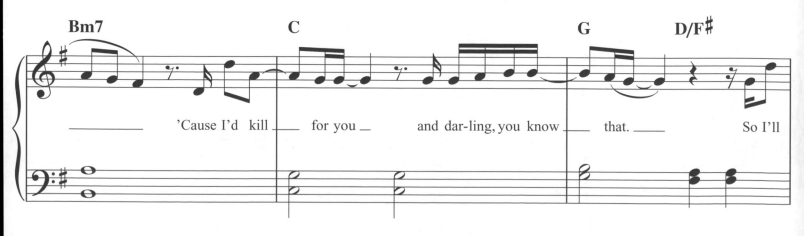

___ _____ 'Cause I'd kill ___ for you __   and dar - ling, you know ___ that. _____   So I'll

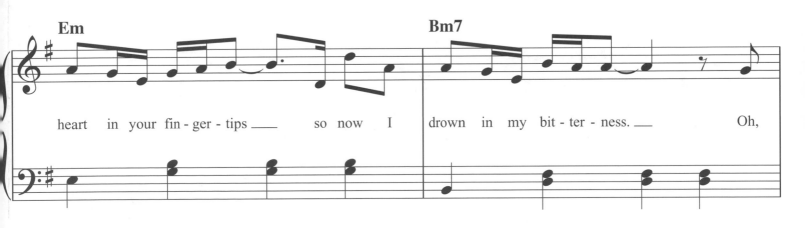

peace.

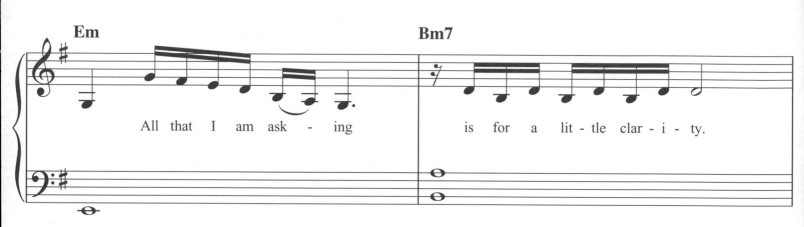

All that I am ask - ing is for a lit - tle clar - i - ty.

That's all that real - ly mat - ters to me. Oh,

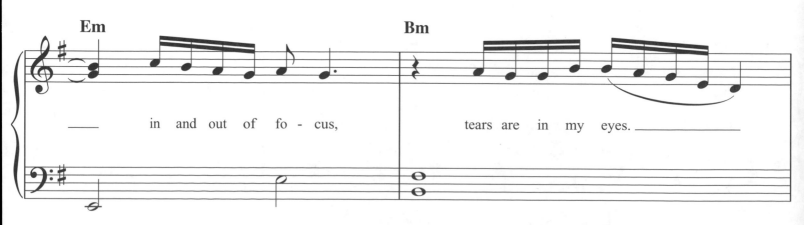

in and out of fo - cus, tears are in my eyes.

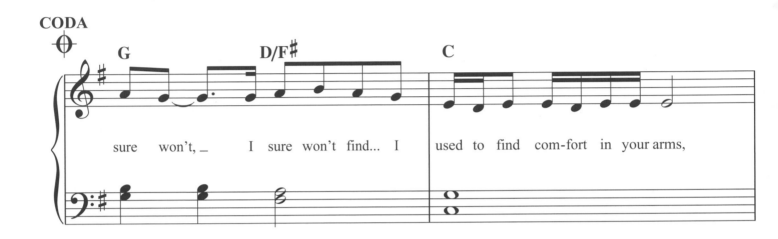

down 'till there's noth-ing left. ___ I sure can't get no sleep and Lord

knows there's no re - lief. You held my heart in your fin - ger - tips ___ so now I

drown in my bit-ter-ness. _ Oh, I can't get no sleep and I sure won't, _ I sure won't find no

peace. Oh, ___ sure won't find ___ no peace, ___ no. ___

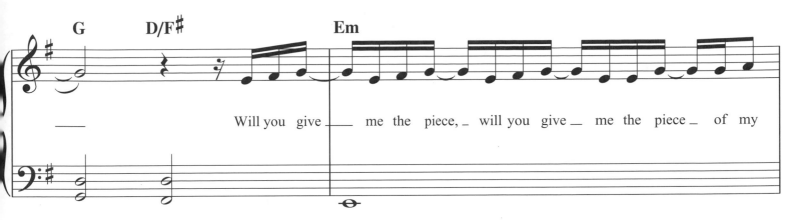

Will you give ___ me the piece, ___ will you give ___ me the piece ___ of my

heart? ___ Will you give ___ me the piece, ___ will you give ___ me the piece ___ of my

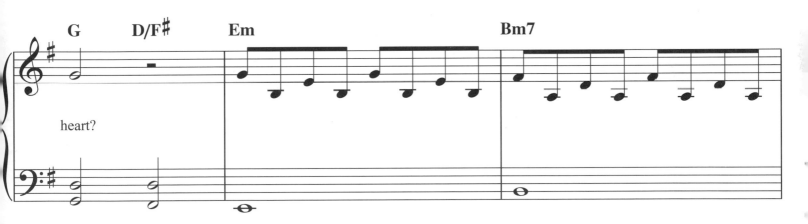

heart?

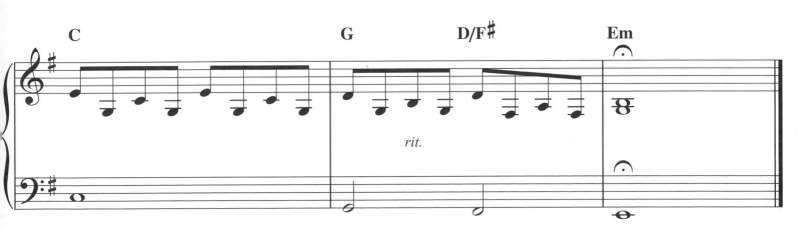

rit.

PALACE

Words and Music by SAM SMITH,
CAMARON OCHS and TYLER JOHNSON

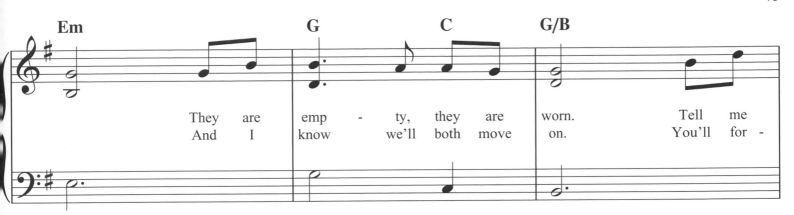

They are emp - ty, they are worn. Tell me
And I know we'll both move on. You'll for -

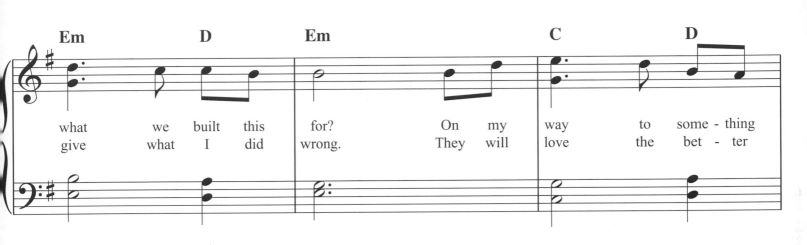

what we built this for? On my way to some - thing
give what I did wrong. They will love the bet - ter

more, — you're that one I can't ig - nore, mmm.
you — but I still own the ghost of you, mmm.

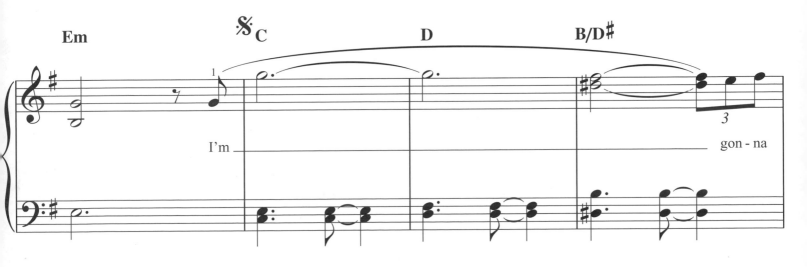

I'm gon - na

46

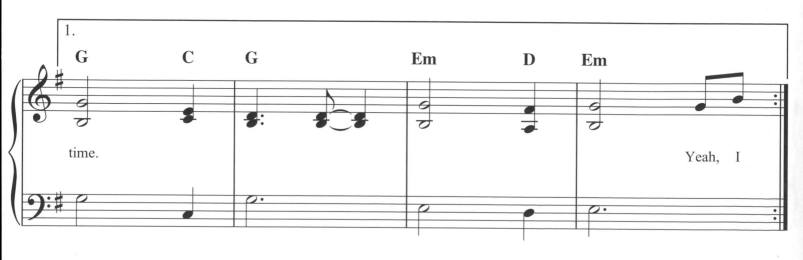

PRAY

Words and Music by SAM SMITH,
JAMES NAPIER, TIM MOSLEY,
JOSÉ VELASQUEZ and LARRANCE DOPSON

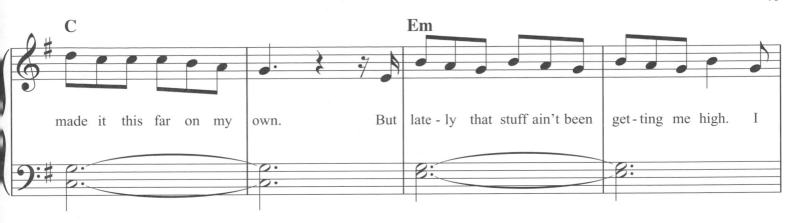

I have nev-er be-lieved _ in you, no, but I'm gon-na pray.

You won't find me in church,

read-ing the Bi - ble. I am still here and I'm still your dis-ci-ple. I'm down on my knees, I'm

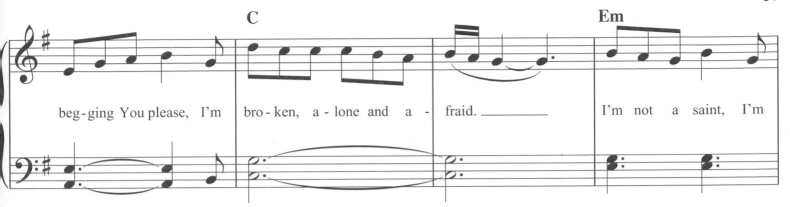

beg-ging You please, I'm bro-ken, a-lone and a-fraid. _____ I'm not a saint, I'm

more of a sin-ner. I don't want to lose, _ but I fear for the win-ners. When I

try to ex-plain, the words run a-way. _ That's why I am stood here to-

day. And I'm gon-na pray, _____ pray. _____

talk a-bout free - dom. Ev-'ry-one prays in the end. Ev - 'ry - one prays in the

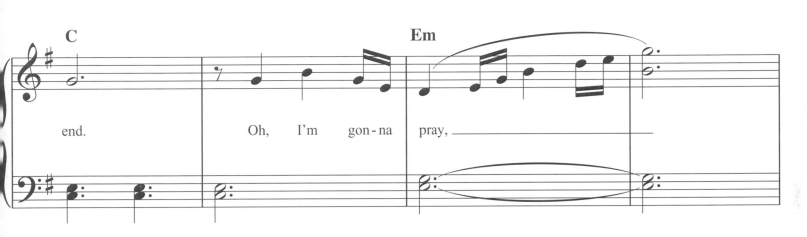

end. Oh, I'm gon - na pray, _____

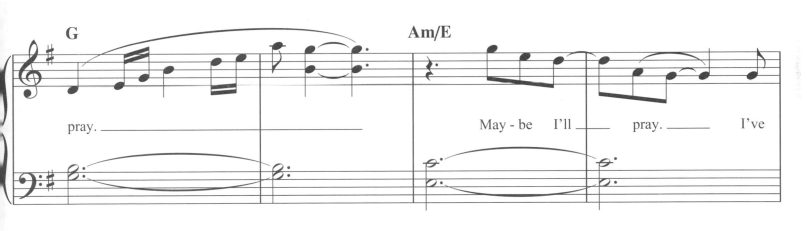

pray. _____ May - be I'll __ pray. _____ I've

nev - er be - lieved _ in You, no, but I'm gon - na pray. _____

rit.

NOTHING LEFT FOR YOU

Words and Music by SAM SMITH
and JAMES NAPIER

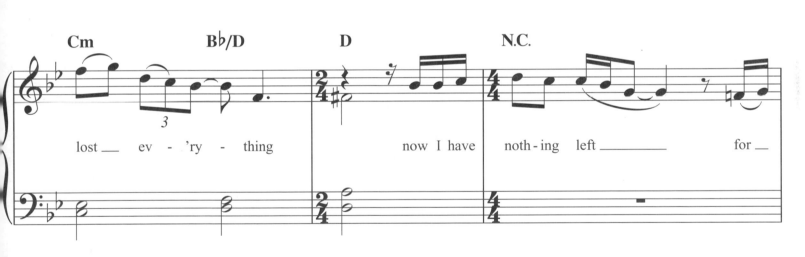

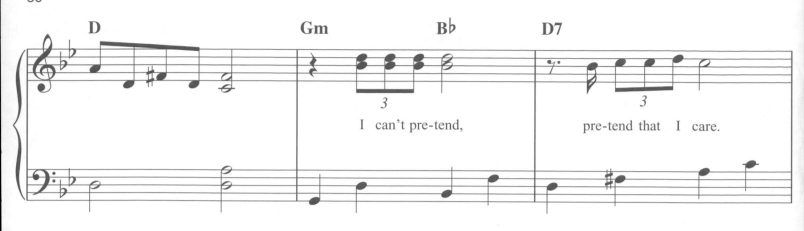

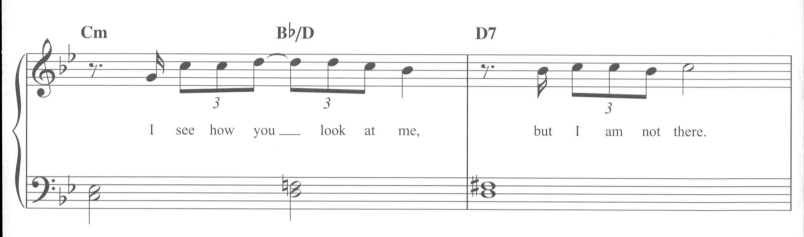

gave my _ heart to a god - damn fool. I gave him ev - 'ry thing, now there's

noth - ing left for you. 'Cause I _____ gave my _ heart

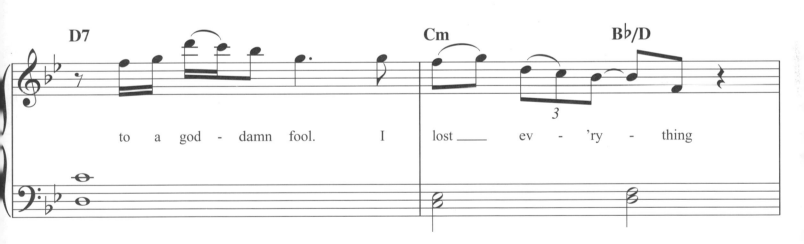

to a god - damn fool. I lost _____ ev - 'ry - thing

and I have noth - ing _ left for... You won't hear me say those words a - gain,

this is some-thing that you can-not mend.   Can't you see I'm a prod-uct of my own

past?   So I know this will nev - er   last. And I will not cov - er your fears,

I will not pick up your tears.   I'll live out the rest of my days a -

lone. _____   'Cause I ___ gave   my   heart

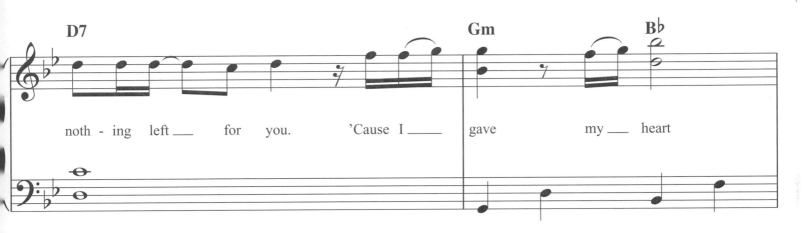

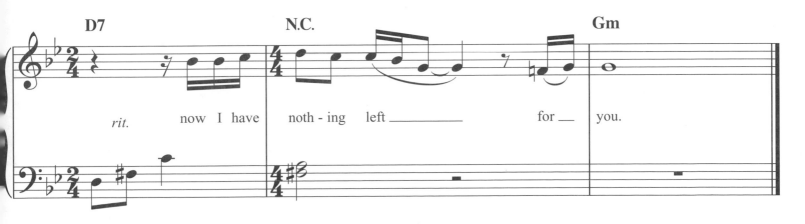

SCARS

Words and Music by SAM SMITH
and BRENDAN GRIEVE

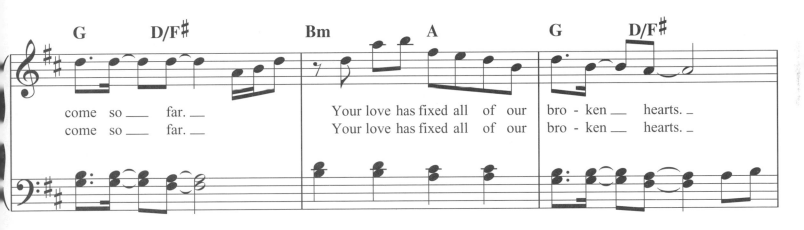

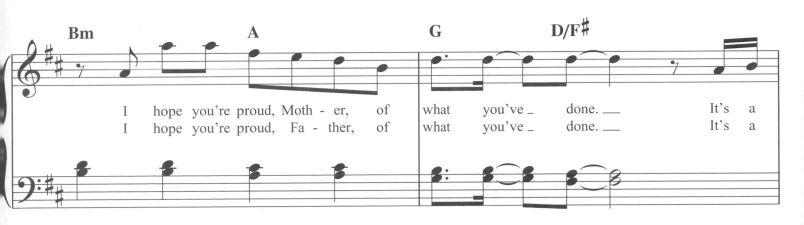

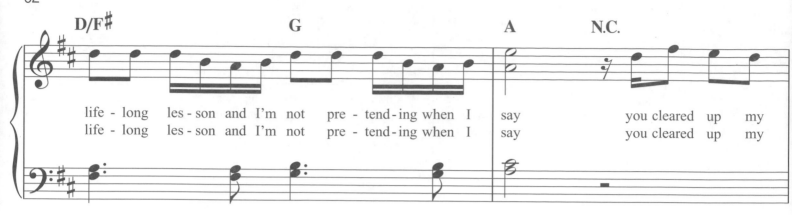

life - long les - son and I'm not pre - tend - ing when I say you cleared up my
life - long les - son and I'm not pre - tend - ing when I say you cleared up my

scars. ___ You ___ cleared up my scars. _____

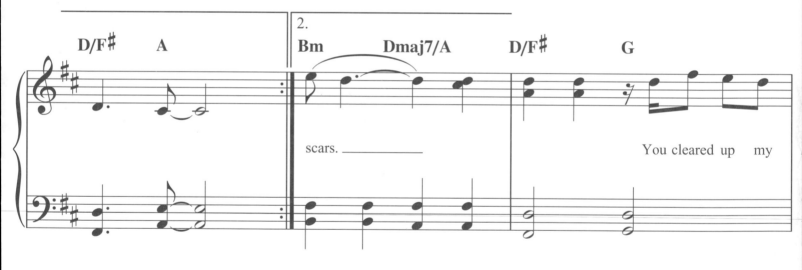

scars. _____ You cleared up my

scars. _____ You cleared up my scars, _____

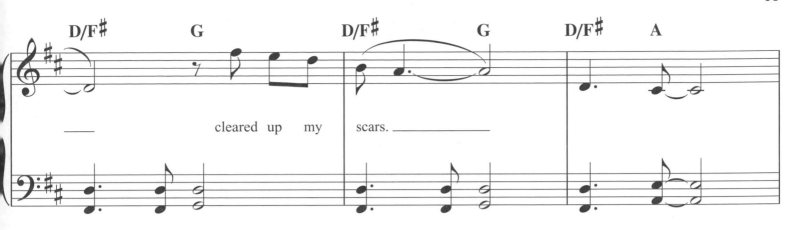

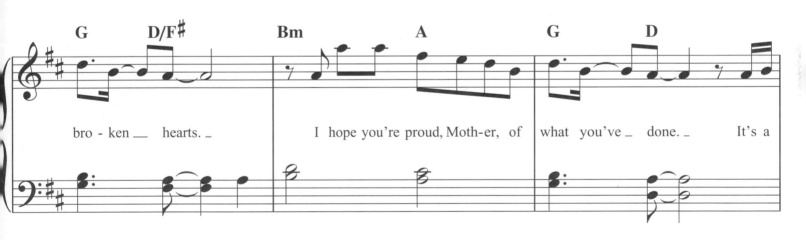

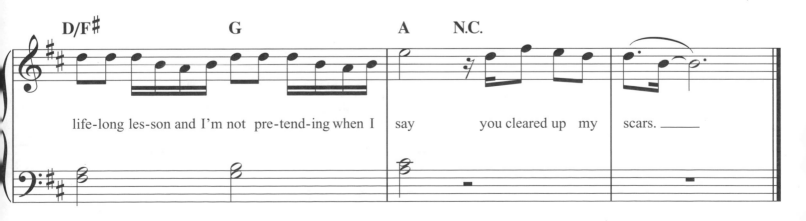

ONE DAY AT A TIME

Words and Music by SAM SMITH
and SIMON ALDRED

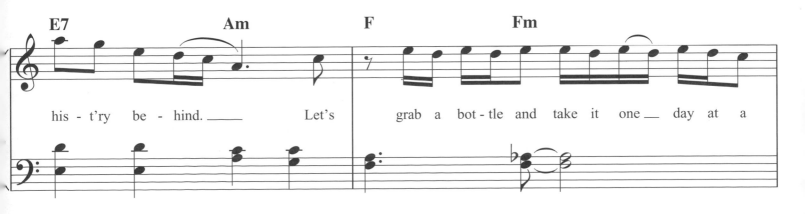

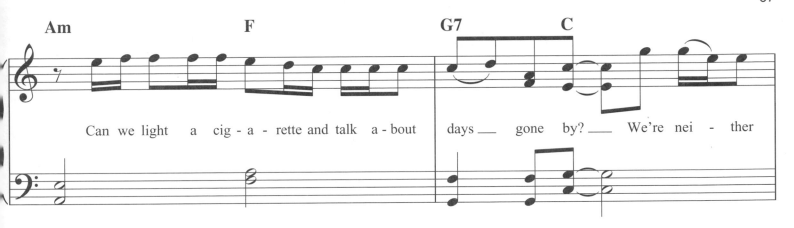

Additional Lyrics

2. I know you're feeling weighed down tonight
   And you can't find the breaks.
   Ev'ry day is too long for you,
   You are sworn to your fate.

   But we got ev'rything we need, baby,
   In the mem'ries we make.
   In a world of reinventions,
   It's never too late.

THE THRILL OF IT ALL

Words and Music by SAM SMITH,
BRENDAN GRIEVE and REUBEN JAMES

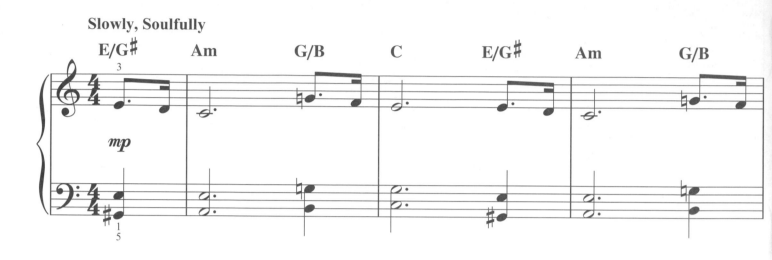

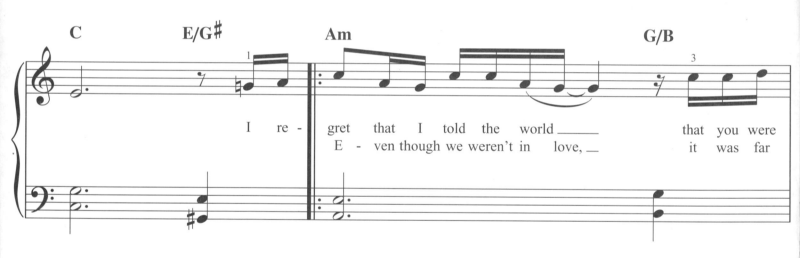

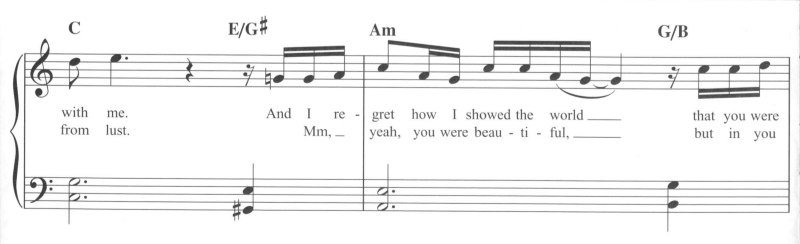

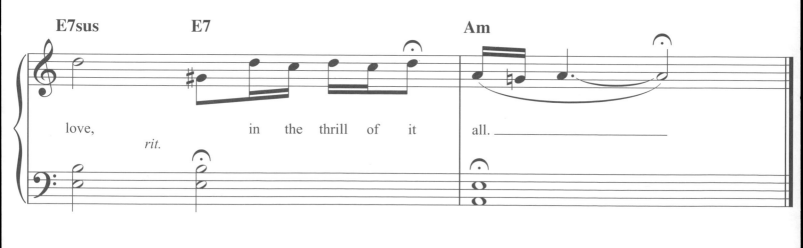